OC

OCCULT MEMETICS

REALITY MANIPULATION

Tarl Warwick 2016

COPYRIGHT AND DISCLAIMER

FOREWORD

When memetics are mentioned the natural inclination of the one witnessing such talk is to either dismiss it as superstition out of hand, or to accept it in the secular sense without relegating any part of the same concept to even slightly, vaguely spiritual fields. It must be said, here, in the foreword of this work, that while memetics is a topic of secular interest (and one of great value in understanding human systems, especially language and propaganda) it ought to be overlapped with the spiritual as I intend here to do, focusing on mainly the direct and indirect applications of the same to the realm of occultism. We must remember that before chemistry came alchemy like Sisyphis and his waxen wings predating human flight.

The fact that people of the alchemical era described what we now know to be rudimentary chemical concepts in spiritual terms roughly equates how memetics is regarded today in some circles as opposed to how it will be described by future generations. The fact that no skilled alchemist ever used spiritual language except as a veil for chemical workings, to get the clergy off their backs and to keep the laypeople from stealing their secretive lore, is clear here. I intend however to forsake this veiling which is still present on modern occult topics and expose it to the wider world for my own purposes.

Memetics is real. Occultism is real. The reader needs first to understand this; it doesn't need to be taken as granted that this is so; properly understood the occult is not black cats, broomsticks, and old women chanting to the moon, but rather protoscientific study as not yet accepted by "mainstream" and secular scientific or cultural forces. The concept of the ability of humans to take flight was once seen identically as impossible, superstitious, and the claim of so many madmen wandering the halls of an asylum.

I will speak of both the basic concept behind, and the various effects of, memetics where they happen to overlap with my own interests; namely in social, political, and strictly occult manners- the rest I will leave out although a tome could be written on those subjects also. The concept of information transference is fairly obvious- speak to someone and you are transferring information to their mind, causing their brain to visualize, often, what you are speaking of. If I describe a red car to someone who has not seen the specific red car, they will visualize it anyways, if they comprehend what "red" and "car" mean, synthesizing material internally within their minds to form an image or idea of what is being described. Through manipulating this tendency to synthesize, memetics in the occult sense is accomplished; this is not the sole manner of the same but is perhaps the most important.

This topic can be used to exert mass social and political change and although previous generations had not quantified the concept, they practiced it nonetheless. It is hidden in plain sight, known formerly to mesmerists and those skilled in rhetoric and philosophy and not to anyone else, and even by those able to use it, still at those times unquantified to any substantial degree.

MEMETICS IS THE SPREAD OF IDEAS

Before memetics in the occult sense is delineated and spoken of in any great detail it must first be understood what memetics actually is. The meme, as proposed by Richard Dawkins (a modern genius in my opinion), is nothing more than a unit representative of a small portion of human culture, spreading and mutating and driving cultural evolution; for indeed everyone has heard of the evolution of biology, but everything extending from biological systems also evolves- behavior, culture, politics, religion, language, everything.

The meme in the modern, standard sense involves typically images, often of a humorous nature which are little more than jokes made viral through the wonders of the internet. This is only one type of meme; often it relates only to the internet subculture of the world, but it can take on much greater importance. I will give some examples in this work later on.

Memetic occultism, then, is the deliberate use of memetics in the otherwise mundane, secular sense, and the manipulation of communication, in order to cause a reflective change in the viewer, listener, or beholder of what is being altered, manipulated, or communicated in a general sense. All propaganda stems from this concept, whether good, bad, or ugly. Newspeak is an example of memetic manipulation. Much of the reality we see around us is shaped by other humans, often long dead, who inadvertently practiced this concept. Much of the rest was deliberately manipulated. Adolf Hitler was nothing more than a master of propaganda who managed to manifest a quasi-reality by manipulating millions of people into thinking the Germanic people were an offshoot of Thule or Atlantis and were destined for European domination and a thousand year reign.

REALITY AS WE PERCEIVE IT IS MANIPULATED CONSTANTLY

The world we see around us is partially the result of observable things and partly the result of our own bias built up like an arcane computer updated constantly with new parts and programs, still functioning in technically the same way as before, but with entirely different opinions about its surroundings, about which it is mechanically aware. Indeed, the human "robot" is an amalgamation of all past civilization, and reality is not perceived the same way by groups which only lately encountered the nearly hegemonic spreading cultures of antiquity as they evolved over time and slowly influenced the entire world during the colonial era.

In the ideology of the early volkish days which came before the bastardization of German nationalism by the latter day Nazi party, in the early 1930s and sometimes before, as an adaptation of the Atlantean and similar philosophies of such minds as Rudolf Steiner and Madame Blavatsky, it was supposed that human beings had lost their collective racial memory through interbreeding but in the process had gained a greater understanding of philosophy, of good and ill, of technology. Steiner's "Occult Significance of Blood" is highly recommended reading for this subject, which in a way, in its content about human understanding, can be considered an early memetic work of note. Sorenson's "Voice of our Ancestors" additionally contributes to this basic premise; when I released an edition of this work some time ago some people questioned whether it meant I was a national socialist- I had to point out that my interest in the work was from this memetic, rather than any racial, perspective and that Sorenson apparently angered Goebbels enough to be imprisoned at one point.

OCCULT MEMETICS

Propaganda is not always negative in form. Often, the very term has extremely negative connotations. At times, it may be utilized by a person or group for what they at least feel is a noble goal; indeed with the exception of propaganda made by corporate or religious entities, it tends to at least have noble purposes behind it as a progenitor- most of those people making propaganda for Stalin believed that communism would work, that it would liberate enslaved peasants, and was a worthy endeavor- one cannot blame them for not seeing the fields of dead Ukrainians in that selfsame era; after all the road to Hell is paved with good intentions. In other cases, good intentions and good outcomes thankfully go hand in hand without such apocalyptic effects.

I have used propaganda against groups before myself; most often against groups already making use of the same for nefarious purposes. Among my targets, over time, have been the now largely irrelevant "Desteni" cult of South Africa (whose members appear to have fallen under the influence of a greedy cult master) and several websites, including, famously, ICQ chat, which was at one point so overloaded by my memetic attacks that people who once detested me for my views ended up working with me side by side, all under the noses, largely, of the people I was targeting in the first place. In both of these cases, only one progenitor- myself- was involved in crafting the material that caused the downfall, partly or completely, of such fronts that I felt were better off in such a lowered general condition. Importantly, memetics was in play in both cases, but in neither case were simplistic subtitled cartoons in the modern sense of a "meme" actually utilized.

SONIC AND SPOKEN METHODOLOGY

Some time ago I created a work entitled "Sonic Occultism; Music as Magick." Within that work I described some of the traditional modes of speech and music and sound in general in a spiritual sense and how it was used over time, especially in advertising. Memetics, paired with speech and music, is particularly potent.

The manipulation of human emotion by the creation of a coherent present narrative (as in a movie, where the scene has to 'come together' fully to have a significant impact on the viewer) relies, often, upon not just what is seen but what is heard; ideas can be transferred without speech. Human minds also place a significance upon gesture (even chimpanzees communicate like this) and symbolism- which makes sense because for the first ten thousand years or so of 'modern' human development either no writing system existed or most of the population was illiterate; at one time, say in Medieval Europe, any town would have had a commercial center lined with stores which bore not a title in script but a symbol of what it pertained to- say an anvil for the local smithy, a cow's head for the stables, a mug of ale for an inn and tavern, a banner emblazoned with swords on the guard barracks, things of that general type.

Strip any movie of its soundtrack and unless it's a gritty *film noir* or extremely minimalist in every aspect, it loses virtually all of its impact. The sound used will differ from genre to genre, and movie to movie. Songs themselves even commercialized in nature, have their own ability to manipulate reality. This is especially potent for people in a time of hardship or stress. Many individuals listen to particular styles of music depending on mood. When I feel down I listen to gothic music and externalize my depression. It works.

OCCULT MEMETICS

When you speak to someone you are transferring information and imagery to their mind. They interpret it as they will, based on what is being said. With some skill you can manipulate their entire worldview in this manner. I will teach you how to do this in a later section to some degree of general aptitude. I offer this general teaching here for academic purposes, since it is already an open secret, so to speak, about how such things may be performed. Most people, though, need a guide specifically speaking of any topic to practice it- which is just as well.

One may think of the occult, or strictly manipulative (another loaded term I do not intend to be universally negative!) variant of memetics as, generally, an attempt to do any of the following:

First, to manipulate the rate and type of spread of an otherwise mundane concept or idea for some spiritual purpose, whether directly or indirectly.

Second, to manufacture concepts or ideas and spread them for some spiritual purpose, whether directly or indirectly.

Third, the inadvertent use of magic directly or indirectly that happens to manifest itself in a memetic sense.

It is helpful here to define magic.

Magic or Magick; What Is It?

Crowley defined magic as "the science and art of causing change to occur in conformity with will" in his third book of 'Magick in Theory and Practice." The most infamous line ever uttered regarding the supernatural, the magical, and the strictly mystical, is "As above, so below" coming from the realm of Hermes Trismegistus. At other times magic appears to be largely defined by (and confined to) Hollywood and apparently involves waving a stick around and controlling lightning or balls of fire in so doing.

I find most of these definitions at best largely unhelpful and at worst outright spurious. I am no fan, myself, of Crowley and most of his work, and prefer a more adequate statement on what magic actually is in my own work; it can be summed up as follows:

Magic is science as yet not quantified and accepted by the reigning, modern ethos of a given society in a given time period.

It might also be defined loosely as *cause and effect by means which are not culturally acceptable, especially within whatever scientific community exists in an era and place.*

These definitions both work much better. When I say "occult memetics" some will immediately ignore the work because they think it involves wearing a black robe and chanting to Osiris or something of that nature. As before, let me mention that alchemy, a magical and heretical practice in its era which got some practitioners burned alive or beheaded, was a chemical art first and foremost over which spiritual terms had been overlapped. In the absence of modern chemistry it seemed truly to be a magical art, and making colloidal gold and similar materials would have seemed miraculous. Any sensible, "rational" modern person of the time period would have either scoffed at it as fallacious and superstitious nonsense, or would have called on the church to rid the community of its practitioners as a den of heretical witches or outright devil worshipers. That they were proto-chemists is of note. This is the case with most science.

OCCULT MEMETICS

The art of sonic magick, which often goes hand in hand with memetics when the memetic practice in question is not solely a captioned image primarily humorous in nature, is of great import in the occult. I practice it often. It has its own memetic force. For example; while one person is best able to use images or written script to spread their ideas or concepts, to the point sometimes of outright propaganda, I myself use sound when the purpose is mostly ritualistic, and video when the purpose is more twain with the secular and the "mundane." I do this because it happens to be something I am more adept at than the use of cartoon images which have been entitled or captioned in such a way as to spread themselves.

Memes Operate on a Biological Principle

Indeed it may be said that when a person practices memetics; whether the information they're trying to disseminate comes in the form of image, video, sound, or written script, they are manufacturing a life form whose entire goal is the same as a life form within biology- that is, the little life form they have made must be able to replicate and spread, as well as reproduce. Like biological life, it also tends to mutate over time. One well made meme, in the sense of an image placed for example on the internet, may spawn thousands of offshoots and entirely new chains of "life" as it spreads, and as it "infects" new human hosts, which either replicate it as-is or mutate it further before spreading it. These ideas and concepts can also infect internet sites, after a manner, for they may be compiled in all their variants on someone's blog and then slowly perpetuate themselves further to other human beings. Indeed, this method of spreading is more akin to an infectious disease than to a standard life form which requires no host- whether the infection is specifically deleterious or possibly even benevolent depends upon the purpose of the maker and the reaction of the new host.

TECHNOLOGY IS NOT THE SOURCE OF MEMETICS BUT IT IS AN AGENT OF THE SAME

Memes in the standard and more well regarded sense technically have existed for as long as the rudimentary trappings of human culture have existed. Being a unit of culture, in some form, they exist wherever human communication able to cause any effect upon the communicated-with party takes place.

The effect of modern technology as it relates to the internet then is the dawn of a new era for humanity just as it is with memetics itself. There have been multiple distinct human epochs of communication and this concept is extraordinarily important if one wishes to fully understand the concept.

The epochs of communication are as follows:

First: Written language. (3000BC) Man, which before spread ideas only through his own actions in a sense of spoken or gestural communication, is now able to lay down his thoughts in semi-permanent form, such that ideas can outlast his life span without an oral tradition and further mutation.

Second: Literary Education. (859 AD) A population that is illiterate cannot make use of written language. Man had to mass-educate the potentially literate population (at first the clerical and upper classes, then the middle class, and finally over time, eventually the entire population) in order to maximize its use.

Third: The Printing Press. (1440s) The ability to produce an order of magnitude more copies of any idea or concept in literary form in a shorter span of time than replicating books by hand, coupled with the protection of its original intent because the mechanical replication of the material was more accurate than any human hand at preserving its content.

Fourth: The Early Industrial Era. (1830s) The rise of the first significant electronic system of communication (the telegraph) finally makes transferring information at distance no longer reliant upon books.

Fifth: Radio. (1894) The rise of the first significant electronic system able to broadcast information without a completely wired system.

Sixth: Television. (1928) Now it is not only sound but also image that is able to be broadcast.

Seventh: The Internet. (1991) With the launch of the first public website, the internet became an eventual repository for virtually all human thought, spanning from far antiquity into whatever modern period is regarded.

Eighth: Modern "Social Media" (2006) Decentralized mass mobilization of the population is now possible. Any individual with a device able to access the internet can spread their ideas and concepts there. Social media represents a new epoch distinct from the internet for the same reason telegraphy is distinct from books despite transferring the same material in a general sense- it is instant in its transference of material. That is to say, each epoch has a sub epoch which makes its full efficiency evident- written language became much more useful when the population had been educated. Electronic systems (telegraph) morphed into much more efficient systems (Radio and TV) and modern computing systems as well with the rise of decentralized media.

SOME IDEAS ARE LITERALLY VIRUSES

Some ideas literally become viral. Sometimes we see the rise of anti-ideas as well. We might consider the concept of black-faxing back in the era where fax machines were still important to the world as an example of this, or any of a number of modern memes on the internet which appear at first to have little or no actual purpose; while I will speak of the concept known as "Dolan" or "Uncle Dolan" as it relates to the spiritual in a later section, the primordial notion of this specific (and often severely degenerated) cartoon was nothing more than a replication of consistently more mutated versions of Donald Duck based on one poorly made drawing of the same which was considered hilarious at the time. Over the course of some months, this meme became almost all encompassing on multiple websites and slowly lost its original meaning, becoming for all intents and purposes nothing more than a repository of lunacy often paired with the worst examples of sexual profligacy, violence, and socially unacceptable content. Indeed, a meme often conveys in a humorous light concepts which are seen as unacceptable for former epochal communication systems- this is almost as important as delineating the epochs themselves; memetics allows the spread of information which is taboo, forbidden, or considered by whatever mainstream zeitgeist exists at the time to be unacceptable subject material- this interacts with the political climate in a large degree.

In the United States, in the early 2000s, the reigning culture was shocked by homosexuality, pacifism, and antireligion. Now, only a little more than a decade later, things have shifted so severely under the current paradigm shift that anti-homosexuality, jingoism, and theism are the new bogeymen haunting the dreams of the pearl clutchers who still cling to their television sets. This is the result of memetics.

14

OCCULT MEMETICS

That those skilled in the use of such memetic propaganda can change entire cultures at a whim with a concerted effort (if they execute such effort over a number of months or years) is here key; this is twain with another concept.

With the rise of each successive epoch of communication (and social media as we see it today will eventually be replaced by something else as well) communication becomes faster, less centralized, more efficient, and more interesting to the average human being. A few decades ago the internet was primarily populated by sites run by a few businesses, colleges, and government groups as well as a few upstart users who wished to pursue a presence there. Now, one generation later, virtually everybody in the Western world and an increasing plurality of people even in the deep parts of the third world has multiple social media accounts, blogs, and similar locations for their sole use; it has become more and more instant in transferring information, and more and more cheap to do so.

Social media will reign until it is displaced by some distinct system which is more rapid and more decentralized. Indeed, the slow march of communication is away from central control and continues to get closer and closer to some sort of anarchic utopia over time. While I happen to chuckle at and disdain anarcho-anything politically speaking, it does seem to work well on social media.

Thus the number of ideas and concepts being generated is now far higher than it was even a year ago, and will be greater next year than it is now. Some of these competing ideas, in various forms, infect new human minds and computer systems over time and replicate in a manner indistinguishable from influenza.

MASS MANIPULATION

Governments know all too well the benefits of being able to control, in a subtle manner, the minds of the population. They have been slightly outflanked, however, by the rapid rise of decentralized communication. It has become difficult for even a large, well funded entity to spread its message in such a competitive environment without resorting to doing whatever it can to keep as many large websites centralized and under their thumb as they can. We might think of a few social media platforms in the modern age which were originally completely anarchic which spawned, internally, a microcosm of authoritarianism by allowing governments to censor information there, often at the behest of tyrannical regimes in theocratic or oligarchic states. Thus, an outlet for their propaganda exists, but they have to be careful with using such power because it has to be presented in a specific manner.

I will elucidate the point; governments do not browbeat their propaganda off on the population at large using social media, because the users thereof- actual human beings- often are turned off to such attempts. Thus, governments, religious bodies, states, and other entities pretend that such propaganda is organically composed and was made by "average people"- this is done through the use of seemingly normal accounts or posters which are actually sock puppets fielded by various agencies or corporations. This was once considered a conspiracy theory until such programs were revealed to actually exist. Even then, with such funding and manpower, this propaganda is largely ineffective on a regular basis except where various entities with often malicious motives behind such acts engage in what amounts to large scale memetic assaults upon the minds of individuals. We see a few notable examples of this happening as this work is being written, with overtones of only the best and most malicious propaganda of the atomic era; namely as an extension of the cold war. Some segments of the world population are being led back into the icy grip of this same decades-long stalemate with all its proxy conflict glory as political entities in the West and East compete for the hearts and minds of an essentially globalized internet. While globalism in the physical world does not work and leads only to the denigration of host and donor states alike, it works very well on the internet, especially with regards to the occult; the stock of spiritual literature now available there comprises virtually every significant occult work from virtually every culture in the world, save for a few primitive uncontacted peoples or the most deep areas of the under-developed world where even electricity is scarce or nonexistent.

It is possible for any random individual to find that a video, image, or text that they have posted, when they arise from bed the next morning, has become a self replicated virus of sorts. This does not happen at random but because of the convolution of different aspects of human culture concerned with its success at replication, the mechanisms behind its reproduction are seemingly so; just as an extremely large ordered mechanism appears to exhibit randomization, an extremely large ordered humanity seems to react randomly to memetics, although this is not the case. Before I delve any further into memetics in this work, it is at this point that I will give two little pieces of advice to those who wish to make use of it consciously; I strongly recommend studying the basics of logic (any textbook dedicated to a decent "Logic 001" course in any college will do.) Second to this I recommend a general understanding of how material on the internet, as a whole or on specific sites, is searched for and found by users; namely, in many cases, through tagging with searchable terms. This is an invaluable fact that most people ignore, limiting their own progress in the process.

THE OCCULT HIDDEN IN PLAIN SIGHT

I would do well here to state something that to occultists will be obvious and to all others will seem incredulous; most often, spiritually significant memetic operations do not take an obviously occult form. They are not demonic sigils or images of wizards chanting to some pagan deity. They take the same general form as any other concept or idea conveyed in this manner. This is not so much by intent as by function; it is simple to explain.

Within memetics, competition in an evolutionary sense exists. Within this competition, some "life forms" die quickly, others replicate for a while, some replicate so well that they spawn mutants which start the same cycle again.

Therefore, an overtly occult image will presumably be spread only by occultists, limiting its number of hosts and hindering its own replication!

Therefore, those occult memes which are not overtly occult but are disguised by design or inadvertently, outcompete the others, spread further and faster, and are more visible. To any observer, occult memetics thus seems a rarity in a field otherwise populated by cat jokes, anime, and political jabs.

It wouldn't even be proper to speak of the materials I myself have put out on the internet in various forms at various times using various websites which have become virus-like in numerous ways. Even most occultists with which I have interacted do not know of my acts in this manner because to reveal this would dampen, perhaps, the effect of further memetic maneuvers. If a person intends only to spread "cute cat" images then making their presence known in doing so helps the

18

replication of these life forms they are spawning. If the purpose is, though, propaganda, remaining hidden is important- which is a concept everybody needs to understand. There is a reason the governments of the world field untold millions of fake profiles all across social media; and it isn't to spread pictures of cats around.

Sometimes a funny meme is just a funny meme

However, most mundane-seeming memes are just that- mundane. No occultism whatsoever is involved with the enormous plurality of cartoons, images, videos, songs, and other materials that spread in a seemingly random arrangement around the internet on a daily basis.

The fact that some otherwise innocuous-seeming materials are tinged by magick and are being used for a spiritual or occult purpose is no different from the same principle being at play with regards to political and social materials- a political concept crafted by a lobbying firm or a group of paid staffers can be represented as though it were created by some random politically-aware teenager somewhere in the middle of nowhere in a flyover state, and by the time anyone can figure out that it was actually the result of a marketing firm and several hour long meetings it's too late and the virus has already spread across the known world.

This shouldn't bother anyone- it is an innate human trait to capitalize upon communication methods and to use them in a manipulative manner; this is not inherently "wrong" or "bad"- you manipulate people every time you haggle about a price, or try to convince them of why your sports team kicks ass and theirs sucks completely. You also manipulate everyone around you with your clothing and your hair style and the presence or absence of makeup, and everything of a similar type.

OCCULT MEMETICS

Virus, Antivirus

Sometimes memetics becomes an actual war. Sometimes, a successful memetic front (a style of cartoon, a specific image, whatever it happens to be) is countered by a competing image or video, or whatever medium it exists in, which has been crafted with the sole purpose of destroying the former. It's a war between viruses where evolution determines who wins. For those adept in the lingo of certain forums and websites, you may equate this to a livelier version of thread or forum sliding.

Let us say that you create a political cartoon of sorts and place it on the internet. People beholding this are absorbing, whether they realize it or not, the idea which it encapsulates. Some of them will laugh and brush it off. Some will find it very humorous or intriguing and perhaps spread it further, others will ignore it. A few people, let's say "me" in this case, deeply dislike your meme, and we want to destroy it.

I will take that image and alter it to invert the meaning of your original encapsulation. Let's say your image is meant to support candidate X and to ridicule candidate Y. But I support candidate Y! I cannot let this memetic affront go unpunished.

My goal here is simple; I am not merely inverting the basic image or the concept of the image but I am attempting to tweak its presentation in such a way that my anti-virus of sorts, my competing party in this miniaturized electronic war, is more effective at replicating itself. This may even grow to such a point at which whenever one of our images is placed online, or our text, or our anything else, the other, its competetive counterpart, is almost instantly placed there too beside or below it by someone else who shares my opinion and dislikes yours.

OCCULT MEMETICS

It then gets down to the nitty gritty; the images, or text, or sound, are competing just like two people locked in a political or religious debate. There are two principles at work here which are of importance to the memetic adept.

First; the image more able to infect human minds will probably win.

Second; at no time is the memetic adept, if they have any intelligence at all, interested in attempting to influence the opinions of the actual other party (in this case, you, the creator of the anti-candidate Y image.) Instead, the memetic adept is competing with this other individual for the opinions of as-yet undecided onlookers.

In a political debate, for example, the purpose of those debating is primarily to influence those watching the debate which have not yet made up their minds. It is far easier to influence these supposedly unbiased parties than it is to rip away those who have already been influenced, especially late in a campaign when cognitive dissonance tends to kick in.

When I debate with anyone I do not structure my arguments and statements in such a way as to convince the opponent- this devolves, usually, into a bunch of personal insults and the audience attention begins to wane. Rather, through a rigorous understanding of the subject and of persuasion, as well as a little bit of appeal to unfortunate human mental processes (like a tendency to react to emotional fallacies) paired with perhaps a more advanced vocabulary than my likely opponent, I will attempt to win over the majority of those participating in a passive manner. This happens on a daily basis as I respond to my critics on the internet (I have many.)

"As above so below" begins to make slightly more sense

when one delves into this general principle; the same biological evolution that drives human competition for resources and mates happens in the internet world on a constant basis. The only substantial difference is that the ecosystem of Earth is finite while the internet, technically speaking, can be expanded infinitely in accordance with new technology. (Arguments about technological limits are irrelevant and I am disposed to ignore them as fallacious.)

Sometimes these little battles between memes are inadvertent; we might think of two popular, viral videos competing for viewers or two images that are both funny, placed on a forum and competing for the top spot in the daily listings of "funniest images of the day" or something of that nature. Often the person who has created a meme, in whatever form it is in, is not even interested so much in significant competition and has merely released it to a circle of contacts or put it on their blog because they themselves find it funny or intriguing, and it spreads from there regardless.

Sometimes these battles are not inadvertent but rather the battle was commenced with purpose. I have engaged in this behavior myself. Here is another secret for the memetic adept; first understand the audience of any particular site and the reigning zeitgeist of that subculture. There is a radical difference, for example, between the audience on a site which is populated largely by outcast groups who are not accepted in the non-technical culture of an era, and a site populated by those who are part of the "in" crowd. This is the same with older technologies, however they are all either irrelevant and dead (telegraphs, AM radio), centralized (older style internet sites), or both (most mainstream television.)

EFFECTS OF MEMETICS: 4CHAN

Ebolachan and Nergal

One of the best earlier examples of occult memetics in action on the internet was largely spawned from (and spread out from) 4chan, specifically its politically incorrect board- a repository and mix of news, analysis, and of course, trolling and shilling.

As ebola began to spread out from Sierra Leone two years ago and as it quickly began ending dozens of lives a day, a general epidemic was declared as occultists descended to declare the risk of Armageddon. As this self fulfilling prophecy continued, and the death toll and rate of death continued unabated, a collective cultural meltdown ensued partially because of the rise of a semi-ironic, semi-realistic cult on the internet (which even got itself spoken of in the African media, the mainstream media, no less) which proceeded to embody the epidemic in the form of a dubiously legal anime character quickly named "ebolachan." This adorable but infectious character was virtually a microcosm of the viral spread of memetics itself, and quickly led to untold hundreds of mutant variants; songs and videos and even sexually depraved stories regarding this insatiable egregore spread around the darker corners of the world to the point at which people began taking pictures of makeshift altars which they put on the internet to frighten and shock people with. That the desire to offend and frighten was central to this specific meme is key. We need however to look at the concept of the egregore or servitor to fully understand the occult implications of roughly twenty thousand deaths resulting from this outbreak, which is technically still ongoing albeit in a slow burning, contained manner.

OCCULT MEMETICS

An egregore is a thought form collectively willed into some semblance of action up to and including semi-sentience. It is inarguable, from an occult perspective, that this process was at work; the collective will was strengthened in a vampiric manner by even the negative reactions of onlookers; namely, the material was so generally offensive that even people with no spiritual beliefs at all replicated the egregore and spread it around by worrying about death cults and by posting on the internet about how stupid the idea of worshiping a deadly virus was.

This was all by design. I fanned the flames myself. Being unskilled in drawing anime (or even crude cartoons) I created a series of videos on the subject where I made sure that my audience was aware that such a movement existed, in hopes that they would look for more information and spread it around further. This was not done to actually cause Armageddon (joking aside) but rather to shock, frighten, and power up other ritualism. I created a series of ambient works loosely related to the same and the ritualism worked quite nicely.

Like a parasite in the guts of a sickened animal, ebolachan caused segments of mainstream culture to consume the same and vomit it back out infecting with even greater speed than the virus itself in its totality. Ultimately, this was the first serious attempt by the occult community to make use of a larger, generally politicized audience for magickal workings, prior workings having been relegated to smaller, specifically occult audiences (on 4chan, the paranormal board /x/, elsewhere, on forums or sites dedicated to similar subject matter.) This basic meme was forced into existence by an organic movement which followed a small amount of prodding.

Kek and Geb

In no way has the experimentation ended with

24

OCCULT MEMETICS

Ebolachan. This riotous affair which threatened to unleash a potentially real plague-style death cult instead ended up being primarily a form of amusement. While I did not invent ebolachan I certainly shaped the egregore to my own will over time, for my own entertainment, without any regard to its ultimate effects; chaos can be fun, and if you believe at all in the concept of cosmic or divine forces, even your most chaotic workings end up subsumed into order, which they in turn have an effect upon- a rather optimistic appraisal of ritualism that might otherwise be considered a failure under any absolutist system.

Enter Kek and Geb, Pepe and Shadilay, and the new era of occult memetics currently ongoing and spreading with ten times the haste of Ebolachan. This second round of memetic force has overrun even the most secular of branches of the boring, tired mainstream media, to the point at which a presidential candidate has in essence "declared war on a cartoon frog" as the more abashed public may term it. Little do they realize this innocuous frog is an egregore of unimaginable force.

I will here give a vague warning that those who do not believe in the occult will probably soon come to realize its reality- this can displace the sense of the mind and lead to a literal breakdown. If you do not believe in magick, do not seek to believe in it- for your adult mind is not capable of regressing to the more pure reality that is in front of you every single day with any degree of ease. I have warned people before; the occult is not dangerous unless one becomes obsessed by it- even inauthentic magic-so-called can be dangerous; consider for example someone who pisses away their savings on lottery games because some oracle or tarot reading compelled them to do so. It can lay waste to you, not because you are infested by demons, but because your actions will not be the same as before. You must learn self control, tactics, strategy and wit.

OCCULT MEMETICS

That being said, I am myself playing a role in the second wave of the second wave of social media occultism; the first wave of release was largely centered around apocalyptic imagery and pestilence. The second ave began with calls for revolution and has tapered off to a much finer point driving social change in a more general sense; Helter Skelter in the philosophical (rather than Mansonian) sense is indeed here.

Synchronicity is an interesting concept. It is a convergence of events and concepts that appears to defy rational explanation as coincidence. We may regard a moment of synchronicity as the result of chaos occasionally converging (shake a jar of water in which are suspended tiny silt particles and at random moments they will meet in groups large enough to seem convincingly conspicuous) or we may regard it as purely occult- either way the occult manifests and influences existence in this manner. The occultist, then, if properly aware of how existence operates, can cause these memetic events through will and action (which must be twain- action without intent is stupid, intent without action is lazy.)

The current synchronicity spreading occult awareness is the result of an apparently organic progenitor- people began to notice that the hieroglyph representing an Egyptian deity called "Kek" strongly resembled a man seated at a computer and a DNA strand emerging from it. They realized that this deity was also represented by a frog, and they quickly determined that this deity was influencing our political system, for political cartoons were more and more often featuring an otherwise mundane cartoon known as "smug pepe"- a frog literally representing smugness encapsulated in image form; the strength of this image of course is the lack of a caption- it needed none, because the image came to represent smug satisfaction in every circle of understanding by pose alone- a gestural, non-verbal meme with significant meaning.

OCCULT MEMETICS

Irreducible complexity matters; it is not possible to simplify this image further because in a completely non-verbal manner it already perfectly expresses a feeling of smugness. How wonderfully this applied to people whose political ideology was gaining dominance, as it still is to this moment. Whether or not the influence of Kek plays a role large enough to topple the reigning world social order via democratic action is as yet unseen, but it will topple it regardless, either that way or some other way- for the egregore is now so powerful it is no longer even contained.

Subsequent to this first wave of spread it was noticed that there was also a band called Pepe, which had produced, apparently, one single album back in the 1980s- this album, of course, included a cartoon frog waving a magic wand. As if it wasn't already enough synchronicity to convince a fence sitter, the length of the one track it contained on its "A" side was 5 minutes, 55 seconds long: 5:55- that Kek is regarded as acting through repeating combinations of numbers, which represent stages between segments of chaos, is key here. This song even seemed, when translated from Italian, to represent what was happening in an occult manner as it overlapped with politics- it spoke of being free, liberated, and being the spawn of rebels and confusion, all very much in play.

I personally dug deeper and realized that 5 in Kaballah (jewish mysticism yes but still a folk rite in itself) was represented by Geburah, and that the numbered name of this sephiroth coincided with concepts such as "young male warriors" (a microcosm of the most significant fan base of the candidate this meme came to represent) and social stress. It was perhaps not coincidental that Geburah is also numbered as 216... or six times six times six. The mark of the beast, how lovely. Thankfully I was never a believer in such practices.

OCCULT MEMETICS

Recently I realized that there was a second Egyptian deity in play- Geb (possibly pronounced "Gek") which is represented by a goose, or duck- funnily, I realized this right after a new scandal in our election broke involving agitators in duck costumes. This deity, of course, was also represented by a hieroglyphic mark that, as I presumed it would be based on my knowledge that the occult is real, appears to depict a man seated once again at a computer with a goose or duck emerging from the same. I made sure to inject this into the awareness of my entire audience on several platforms because I realized it as a significant synchronistic mark of things to come.

Never in my life have I seen any time period marked by so many examples of clear-cut synchronicity. I could, even as an occultist, ignore a coincidence or two, but three coincidences each marked in turn by a half dozen or more minor coincidences seems to be the hallmark of a more substantial event and concept. I have to believe that forces were unlocked by our former dabbling that caused this situation to arise; now, chaos takes hold and events spiral on as they will, agitated by the collective will of thousands of occultists and millions or tens of millions of others beholding the same workings.

MEMETIC TACTICS OF NOTE

Irreducible complexity is the first and foremost topic of note within the actual use of memetics. Keep it simple. There is a time and a place for lengthy exposes on video, and then there are times and places for something simple. Think of what I have spoken of regarding that most smug of frogs and his equally irreducible counterpart, Wojak, also known as "feels bad"- this separate entity, twain with the former, represents regret, sadness, and a feeling of general discomfort, especially in an empathetic way.

OCCULT MEMETICS

If the meme is an image it should be simplistic. If it is uncaptioned let it evoke a feeling such that it is able to be used in virtually any situation. It if is captioned, the caption ought to be simplistic, unless the goal is an ironic attack upon an already simplistic meme image, in which case it ought to be overly complicated to a humorous degree.

If the idea being conveyed is textual let it be as short as it is able to be while conveying the idea- the audience should be considered vast, so it must be preferably in English, and preferably at a lower-than-collegiate reading level. No big words unless it is being used to imitate or mock "high brow" speaking patterns (see Joseph Ducreaux).

If the conveyance is in video form the speaking ability of the occultist is of greatest import. What is said matters little. One can speak for an hour and the audience will either be entranced entirely the whole length, or pay attention predominantly only to the very beginning and very end, which is where respectively the hook and the summation shall be placed.

An idea will not spread if it cannot be translated. If I tell a Yanomami warrior from the middle of the jungle about snow the closest approximation in his language for the concept I am expressing is probably "a rain drop that no longer has heat like a fire does" or something of that nature. This is perhaps the biggest stumbling block to success in memetics. We all know "that person who didn't get it" when we told them a joke that they simply did not translate properly. Their improper understanding probably kept them from getting it as they mouthed it to themselves several times, before they finally gave up, pretended to understand it, and giggled in an uncharacteristically hyperactive manner. Either that or you had to prod them on and explain it at length, to yours and their chagrin.

OCCULT MEMETICS

One should also be aware that there is a hierarchy of human understanding and its inverse meaning as it pertains to importance. The human is driven first by the visual, and thus the visual is prime, and the reaction to images will invoke great emotion if properly fitted, but inversely it will be the most difficult to encapsulate meaning in image alone (whether a picture or a video without sound.) The human sees next, and thus it becomes a bit easier to evoke a response but a bit less of a response overall. The necessity of the human mind to do more complex interpretation with text means it causes the least response but causes a response the most easily- the brain has to translate the text into image and sound mentally. "Touch" can also be memetic although it must be transferred manually person to person, the one exception being extremely high bass levels in sound waves, which cause a significant response of their own, properly formatted.

Let the spiritual be veiled as it is in alchemy. Explicit spiritual overtones cause an explicit spiritual effect but this variant has a smaller audience to replicate it. Rather, replicate the image first, and then describe the significance thereafter in a sort of two step system. This is how Kek came into being on our plane of existence. It works. Hide away the meaning until you are prepared to unveil it, and then do so in a textual, descriptive manner able itself now to replicate, piggy-backing off of the image which was formerly seen only as amusing or utilitarian (it stands in for a reaction, usually emotional or quasi-emotional.)

Finally, keep in mind that your creation will need to compete. If at first it does not succeed, tinker with it. Experimentation that leads to consistent positive effects is far easier than attempting to expend ten times the effort to force an ineffective spiritual meme into replicating at a sustainable level.

REALITY IS SUBJECTIVE IN HUMAN SYSTEMS

If I tell you that the sky is blue I have just made an objectively true remark upon its color. At the same time, I have made a subjectively true remark. How can this be?

The answer is simple; the term we use for the color of the sky, as we, as humans, describe it (assuming the other party is speaking English and it isn't stormy or night time out) is blue- within the framework of human understanding, which is subjective, the statement is objective fact. It exists within the human framework only, that color has no significance beyond our observation. In reality it's just emitting a certain wavelength of what we know to be anthropically observable light. This is, anyways, how we describe it, again within our subjective understanding of the world.

All of our communication is subjective. The term "racism" did not exist anywhere in the human lexicon until modernity. Before it was invented to describe a concept there was no conception of the same. One could have gotten close with, perhaps, bigotry or something of that nature, or perhaps "hate" in a general sense, or aversion. Whenever a constructed term has been made to fill in human understanding, the gaps therein that is, it is a loaded term, regardless of its function. I state this not to say that human understanding is bad or wrong, but because this is, again, within our framework, absolute truth. When we remark that "the egg is white" it has no significance beyond human understanding. I have often thought about this general subject and decided after a while that it was the most important occult topic of all.

OCCULT MEMETICS

When memetics is engaged in the biological component of the replication process is a perfect microcosm of human biology. The descriptions of this concept are a perfect microcosm of the descriptions we make of ourselves and, through our communication, everything else we witness. Our reality is not objective- no two humans ever observe the same thing. There is a simple experiment that can prove this. Cut an apple in half, and position it in a flat plane (a piece of wood, or whatever) and hold the full half of the apple up to someone so that they are unable to see the fact that the other half is gone. Ask them what they see.

"An apple" they will reply.

It isn't an apple, it's half an apple- the discreet thing they are seeing only resembles an apple because they are not aware of the other half being gone. In some other reality we might consider halves-of-apples as discreet units and what we call in this reality a full apple to be merely "two half-apples." This is a profoundly important statement on reality; it isn't even real.

References to artificial reality aside, this has an impact on memetics. People will often see what they wish to see. It happens in human psychology especially when significant emotion is involved. Thus, the candidate you like is flawless even when flawed, and their flaws excused through cognitive dissonance, while the other candidate, that you do not favor, is of course a reincarnated Adolf Hitler or Joseph Stalin. Anyone who does not agree with your worldview is likely to either be an antiquated old bag or a young clueless punk, anyone who stands in your way deserves it when you crush their ambitions.

This is all part of the grand chessboard of reality- the macrocosm upon which the infamous nuclear grand chessboard exists. Learn this lesson well and you can manipulate reality however you wish simply by being convincing. Today's madman is tomorrows religious founder or nations' father. The lunatic rambling about conspiracies may indeed be correct. The madman and the visionary are ultimately separated only in that the madman has not yet convinced enough other people that his madness is correct and provides a framework upon which to understand reality. The visionary is just a madman with enough persuasion skills to convince a large enough audience that his own lunacy is reality.

HOW I DESTROYED ICQ CHAT

I offer this segment of the work only to illustrate the basic concept of propaganda as opposed to claiming it has any significance of great note; indeed, by the time I was using this chatting service back in 2007 it was already beginning to wane, and within a half decade much of it was empty. For those without a general understanding of IRC chatting services or internet culture at large, you will probably have to research what I'm talking about here. I strongly recommend the ICQ christianity blog (but I may be biased since I was the one archiving the content there.)

Like I have described, my goals were noble; I was there to enjoy myself and faced nothing but flak from those empowered on the site to stifle speech they did not like. As a proponent of Luciferian liberty I felt it was just cause enough to fight back, and so I developed a cunning long term campaign that I knew would inevitably lead to victory. I say this not to be worthy of cringing- I admit openly that such a thing is unimportant, merely I claim it is a microcosm of how propaganda operates.

I began running everybody down, including those who I spoke with amicably. I gave everyone on the service stockholm syndrome as I came back to attack over and over again like a complete nut. On this primitive IRC chatting service it was nigh on impossible for anyone, even those in total control of the website, to keep me out for more than a few minutes at a time. Phase two then commenced.

Once a segment of the people there, through my incessant acts of perturbation, had come to accept my vision of reality- that those in charge of the site were biased and inept- I had planted the seeds of its undoing. I quickly began speaking much more softly to this segment of the population there, slowly convincing them that we were part of a movement to liberate the site. It didn't matter that the claim was foolish- they had stockholm syndrome by then and had grown to identify with me.

Then I unleashed Hell on the website as I called for backup- over a few months the site was largely emptied of users, because the same ban-happy bias I had told people of before was now being reinforced by the day to day grind of nonstop attacks. Even those who disliked me began to complain that those in charge were inept and biased- inept because they were perceived of as powerless to stop the onslaught, biased because regular users often got swept aside during such raiding activity. Lo and behold, now even my former enemies were saying the same exact things I said to begin with. It wasn't long before the administration that managed the site abandoned ship in rage. The only negative effect was that the service was, several months later, destroyed altogether by the owners of the site at large- but by then it didn't matter because the website was overrun. I won in the end because I managed to polarize the population and then eventually turn my enemies into doppelgangers of myself, communication-wise. Understand this section well and you should be able to replicate this success; plan ahead for your campaign and never surrender.

CONCLUSION

Of all occult practices memetics is the one of greatest import in human systems. Through manipulating human understanding virtually every religion has emerged. Each religion is nothing more than the overthrow of a previous system because someone arose and made a more compelling case for their own version of reality.

This little manuscript covers some of the more important fundamental topics within the general lexicon of memetics as a whole only insofar as it relates to propaganda and occultism- memetics are in play even in the most secular of human affairs, driving human culture itself as a vehicle of human understanding. While technically speaking these workings are theoretical there is no theory needed for the spiritual world; the basic concept of altering reality at a whim is the very essence behind the archetype of the shape shifter, and even of the witch or wizard, able to act out any role as literal cosmic method actors. The gods and goddesses of old, too, transformed themselves at times, and the minds and pens of man transformed them as well through their art, their words, and their stories on tablets, and scrolls, books, and now blog posts as well.

Much like antiquated mages in olden days with magickal clay tablets must have thought that those "new age scroll users" were inauthentic there will be the tendency to remark that the internet is so new, and technologically adept, that it is senseless to compare it with the occult, or with magic, which all adults, after all, "know" is "not real." So too did people listening to their spooky radio broadcasts later spurn the same horror flicks on television that younger audiences were captivated by.

THE END

Made in the USA
Monee, IL
17 December 2021